# Get to know Screws

By Paul Challen

## Crabtree Publishing Company

www.crabtreebooks.com

# Crabtree Publishing Company
## www.crabtreebooks.com

**Author:** Paul Challen
**Editors:** Molly Aloian, Reagan Miller, Crystal Sikkens
**Project coordinator:** Robert Walker
**Prepress technicians:** Ken Wright, Margaret Amy Salter
**Production coordinator:** Margaret Amy Salter
**Cover design:** Samara Parent
**Coordinating editor:** Chester Fisher
**Series and project editor:** Penny Dowdy
**Project manager:** Kumar Kunal (Q2AMEDIA)
**Art direction:** Dibakar Acharjee (Q2AMEDIA)
**Design:** Ritu Chopra (Q2AMEDIA)
**Photo research:** Farheen Aadil (Q2AMEDIA)

**Illustrations:**
Q2AMedia Art Bank: pages 6, 7, 12, 14, 15, 22, 23

**Photographs:**
Corbis: Koopman: p. 26
Dreamstime.com: Jstudio: p. 5; Homestudiofoto: p. 10;
   Ijansempoi: p. 17 (bottom left); Kmitu: p. 18 (top);
   Berean: p. 21; Thomas Perkins: p. 25; Denis
   Radovanovic: p. 27 (top right); Monkey Business
   Images: p. 27 (bottom right)
Fotosearch: Central Stock: p. 13
Time & Life Pictures/Getty Images: p. 28, 29
Ingram photo objects: p. 4 (lever)
Istockphoto: p. 19; Clayton Hansen: p. 4 (wheel and axle)
Photolibrary: Richard Hutchings: p. 16
Shutterstock: p. 18 (bottom); Medvedev Andrey:
   p. 4 (screw), 9, 31; Andrjuss: p. 4 (wedge); Julián
   Rovagnati: p. 4 (inclined plane); Harley Molesworth:
   p. 4 (pulley); Yari: p. 8; dragon_fang: p. 11; Juriah
   Mosin: p. 17 (right); Richard Lister: p. 20;
   Medvedev Andrey: p. 24; Vaclav Volrab:
   p. 27 (bottom left)

**Library and Archives Canada Cataloguing in Publication**

Challen, Paul, 1967-
   Get to know screws / Paul Challen.

(Get to know simple machines)
Includes index.
ISBN 978-0-7787-4469-6 (bound).--ISBN 978-0-7787-4486-3 (pbk.)

   1. Screws--Juvenile literature.
I. Title.  II. Series: Get to know simple machines

TJ1338.C43 2009        j621.8'82        C2009-900796-7

**Library of Congress Cataloging-in-Publication Data**

Challen, Paul C. (Paul Clarence), 1967-
   Get to know screws / Paul Challen.
      p. cm. -- (Get to know simple machines)
   Includes index.
   ISBN 978-0-7787-4486-3 (pbk. : alk. paper) -- ISBN 978-0-7787-4469-6
(reinforced library binding : alk. paper)
   1. Screws--Juvenile literature. I. Title. II. Series.

TJ1338.C44 2009
621.8'82--dc22
                                                        2009004586

## Crabtree Publishing Company
www.crabtreebooks.com        1-800-387-7650

**Published in Canada**
**Crabtree Publishing**
616 Welland Ave.
St. Catharines, ON
L2M 5V6

**Published in the United States**
**Crabtree Publishing**
PMB16A
350 Fifth Ave., Suite 3308
New York, NY  10118

**Published in the United Kingdom**
**Crabtree Publishing**
White Cross Mills
High Town, Lancaster
LA1 4XS

**Published in Australia**
**Crabtree Publishing**
386 Mt. Alexander Rd.
Ascot Vale (Melbourne)
VIC 3032

# Contents

# What is a Simple Machine?

All people have jobs to do. Some jobs take a lot of **energy**. Energy is the ability to do work. **Simple machines** help people get jobs done without working too hard. This is called **mechanical advantage**.

Simple machines are tools that are made up of very few parts. There are six kinds of simple machines. They are **inclined planes**, levers, pulleys, wedges, **screws**, and wheels and axles.

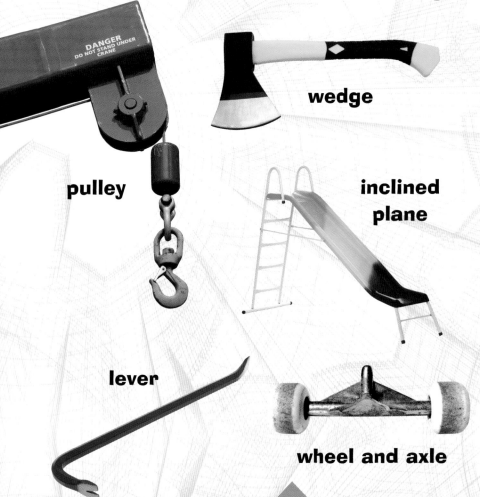

**pulley**

**wedge**

**inclined plane**

**lever**

**wheel and axle**

**screw**

These pictures show an example of each kind of simple machine.

A screw is a simple machine that is made from another simple machine. A screw is an inclined plane that is wrapped around a **cylinder**. Screws are used to lower and raise things. Screws are also used to hold objects together.

Screws are all around you. You can see screws on a lightbulb, a lid of a jar, and a key ring.

# Wrap It Up!

This activity will show you how a screw is made. You will need:

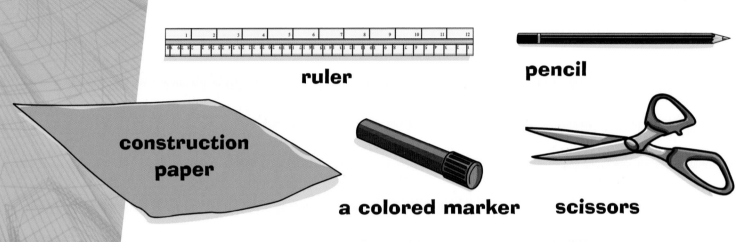

**ruler**  **pencil**

**construction paper**  **a colored marker**  **scissors**

Use a pencil and a ruler to draw a right triangle, like the one shown here. Next, use your scissors to cut out your triangle.

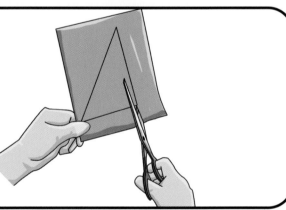

Use your marker to color the longest edge of the triangle.

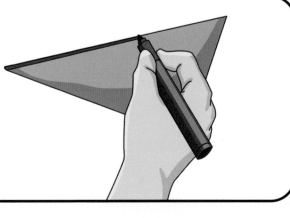

Place the shortest side of the triangle along the side of the pencil.

Roll the pencil and paper together.

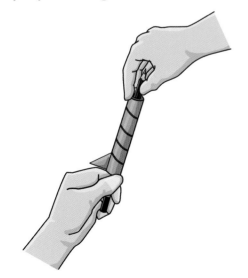

Notice how the edge you colored with marker wraps around the pencil in a **spiral** pattern.

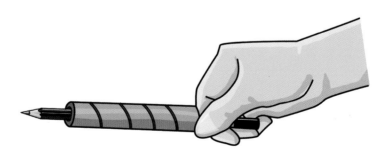

# Parts of a Screw

A screw is not smooth like a nail. A screw has ridges around it. These ridges are called **threads**. The threads help move the screw forward or backward.

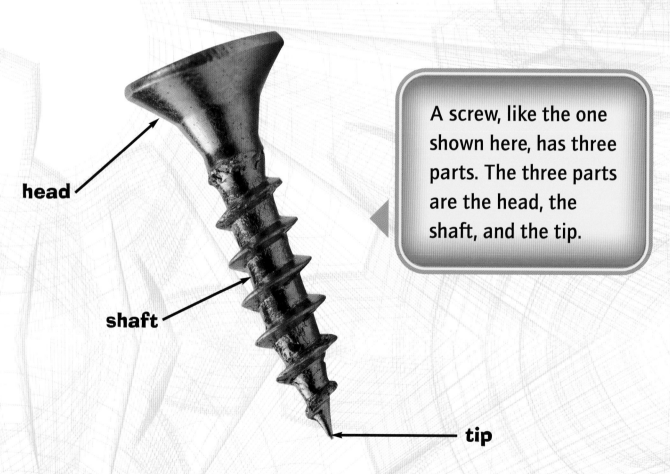

head

shaft

tip

A screw, like the one shown here, has three parts. The three parts are the head, the shaft, and the tip.

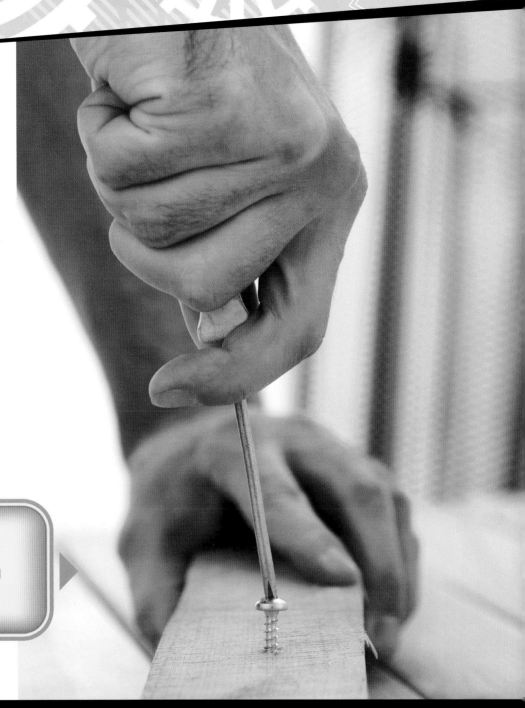

This person is using a screwdriver to lower a screw into the wood.

Force is the push or pull on an object. All simple machines need force in order to work. For example, a screwdriver applies force to the top of the screw. This force drives the screw into an object.

# How a Screw Works

You use screws everyday to fasten things together. You can see a screw in action every time you fasten or unfasten the lid of a bottle or jar. The lid of a bottle or jar is a screw. The lid has threads. The opening of the bottle or jar also has threads. When you turn the lid, the threads on the lid fasten or unfasten to the threads around the opening.

**threads**

This girl is applying force to the lid of the jar to unfasten it.

# Fastening and Joining

A **bolt** is a type of screw. It has a flat tip. A bolt creates a strong connection between two objects. Sometimes a **nut** is added to the end of the bolt to make the connection even stronger. Bolts and nuts are used in cars, buildings, and bridges.

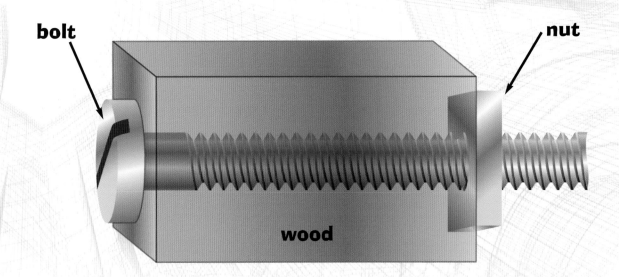

bolt

nut

wood

This nut and bolt combination prevents the bolt from coming loose.

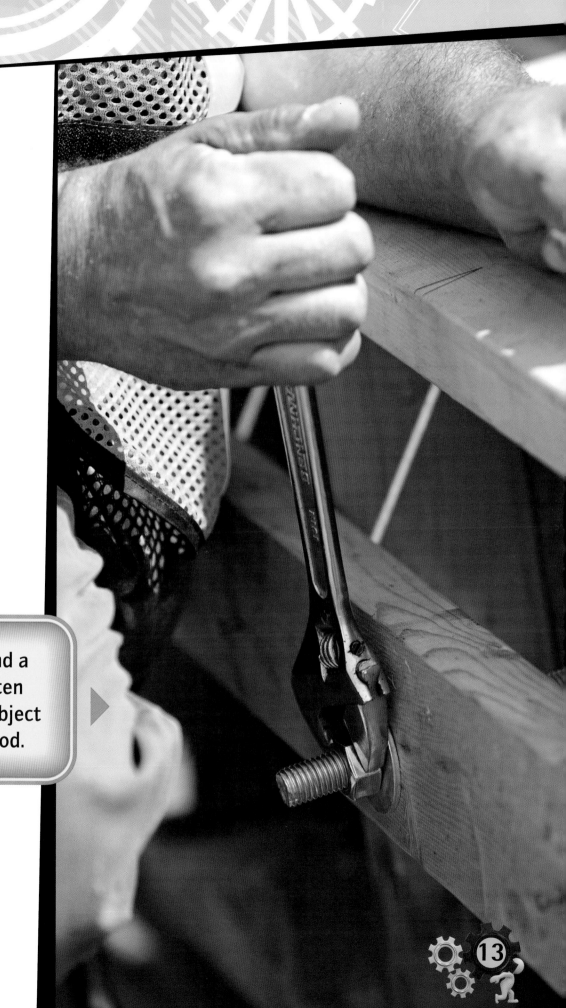

A nut turns around a screw to help fasten the screw to an object like a piece of wood.

# Fun with Fastening!

This activity will show you how a screw and a nut join to form a powerful connection.

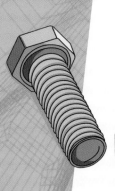

**a bolt and nut combination**

## Step 1

Place the nut on the bottom of the bolt.

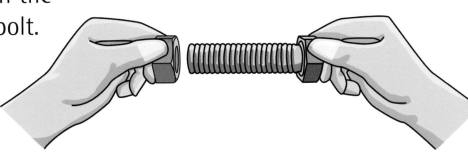

## Step 2

Holding the bolt still, turn the nut so it begins to fasten to the bolt. Which way do you have to turn the nut so that it makes the "connection?"

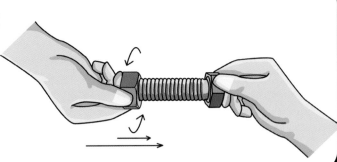

14

Now turn the nut in the other direction so that it moves down the bolt. Keep turning the nut until it is at the bottom of the bolt.

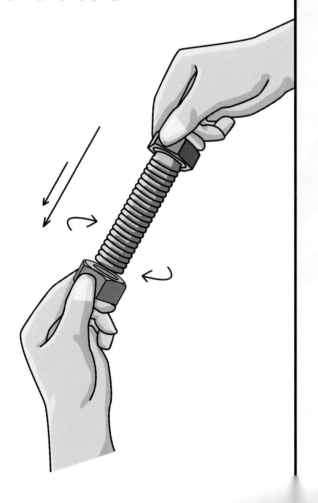

Now, hold the nut still and turn the bolt. Which direction do you turn the bolt to make a connection? To tighten a screw, you turn it to the right. To loosen a screw, you turn it to the left. Here is a fun way to remember which direction to turn a screw: "Righty tighty, lefty loosey!"

# Raising and Lowering

Screws are also used to raise and lower objects. For example, some stools use a screw to raise or lower the height of the seat. The seat is attached to a large screw. By turning the seat, the height of the stool raises or lowers.

A car jack has a long screw. By turning the screw, the jack raises or lowers. A car jack is used to hold a car in place while a person changes the tire.

**screw**

**car jack**

# Other Uses of Screws

Screws are also used to pull apart objects. For example, a corkscrew is a tool used to open bottles. A corkscrew is used to pull out the cork from a bottle. A hand drill is another tool that uses a screw. A hand drill is used to make holes in wood.

The threads of a screw cut into an object, such as wood or cork. As the screw lowers, it pushes the material up, leaving behind a hole.

An oil drill breaks through hard rock to reach oil found deep under the ground. Using an oil drill requires much less work than digging by hand.

# Screws and Screwdrivers

A screwdriver is a tool used to turn a screw. Turning the screwdriver applies force to the screw. The force drives the screw into an object. The screwdriver's tip fits into the shape on the head of the screw. This helps the screwdriver grip tightly to the screw.

This screwdriver and screw fit together to make it easier to drive the screw into the wood.

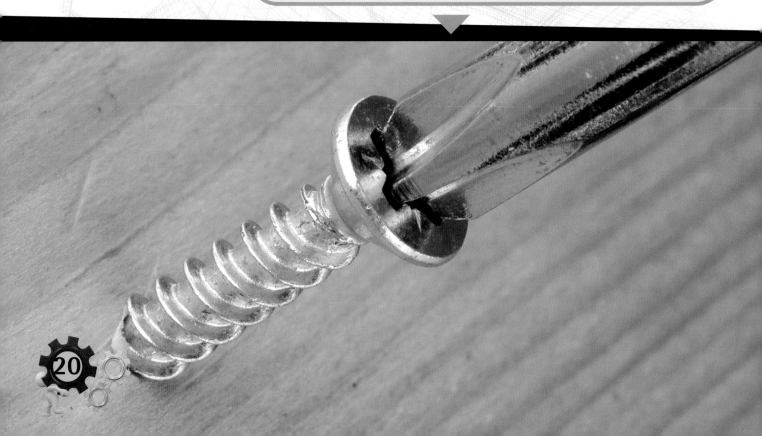

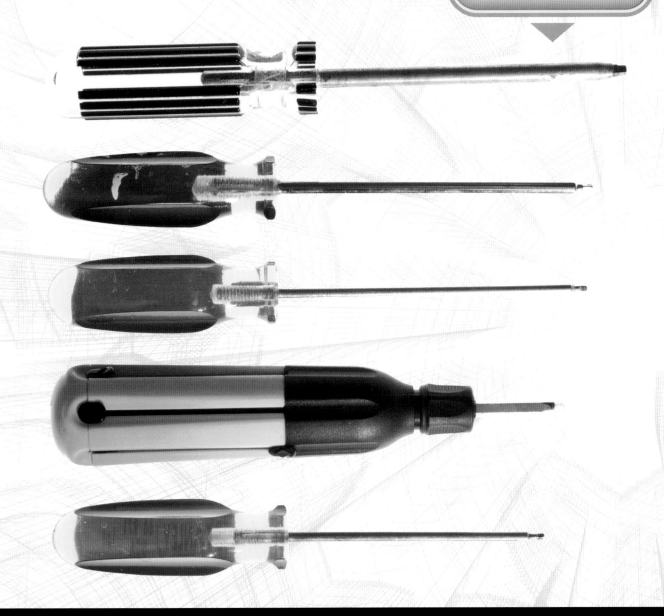

The Robertson screwdriver has a square tip.

The Robertson screw and screwdriver were named after the Canadian inventor, Peter L. Robertson. Robertson invented this screw and screwdriver in 1908.

# Working with Screws

This activity uses a screw and a nail to compare force and time. You will need:

**firm modeling clay**

**a two-inch (5 cm) screw**

**a two-inch (5 cm) nail**

Push the nail into the modeling clay, using as much force as you can.

Now, twist the screw into the modeling clay, using as much force as you can.

Which took more force to push into the modeling clay—the screw or the nail? Twisting the screw into the modeling clay used less force than pushing the nail. Pushing the nail into the clay, however, took less time than twisting the screw.

less force = more time
more force = less time

# Finding the Pitch!

Some kinds of screws have a lot of space between their threads. Other screws have little space between their threads. The space between the threads of a screw is called **pitch**. A screw with threads that are close together has a small pitch. A screw with threads that are far apart has a large pitch.

Look closely and you will see different screw pitches.

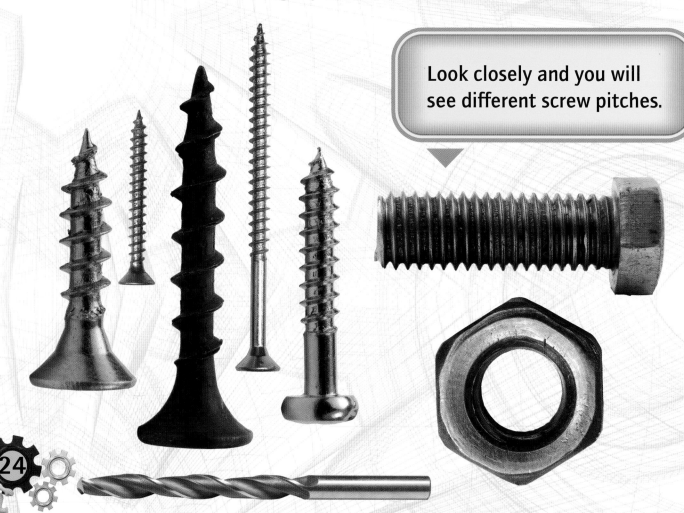

How many more turns will it take to finish driving this screw into the wood?

Think about using a screwdriver to drive a screw into an object. Each time the screw turns, it moves down one thread. Count the number of threads on a screw to find out how many turns it will take to drive the screw into the object.

25

# Simple Machines Working Together

Simple machines can work together. A machine made up of two or more simple machines is called a **complex machine**. Many complex machines include screws.

A pencil sharpener is a complex machine. Many parts move together to do work. A wheel and axle turns screws inside the pencil sharpener. The screws sharpen the pencil.

All of these complex machines have screws. Look around your home and school for other complex machines that use screws.

# The History of Screws

The screw was invented many years ago. Screws were first used to help with farming. A man named Archimedes invented a screw to help farmers lift and move water from rivers to fields. The screw is inside a large cylinder. One end of the cylinder is placed in the water. By turning the screw, water is lifted from the river through the cylinder and out the other end.

The screw that Archimedes invented helped farmers water their crops.

**Archimedes, often called the "inventor of the screw," was a Greek scientist.**

# Glossary

**bolt** A screw with a flat tip that's commonly fastened with the help of a nut

**complex machine** A combination of two or more simple machines

**cylinder** An object that is solid or hollow and is shaped like a tin can

**energy** The ability for doing work

**inclined plane** A flat or level surface set at an angle

**mechanical advantage** How much easier and faster a machine makes work

**nut** A fastening device that has circular hole with a thread inside that combines with a screw (bolt) to make a tight connection

**pitch** The distance between two threads on a screw

**screw** A simple machine used to raise and lower objects, or hold them together

**screwdriver**  A device that fits in the head of a screw and is used to turn a screw more easily

**simple machine**  A tool that makes work easier by spreading out the work needed to move a load

**spiral**  A winding curve

**thread**  The ridges around the shaft of a screw

# Index

# Web Sites

www.ehow.com/how-does_4600493_a-screw-work.html

inventors.about.com/od/sstartinventions/a/screwdriver.htm

www.fi.edu/qa97/spotlight3/screwdemo.html

www.collectionscanada.gc.ca/cool/002027-2008-e.html

math.about.com/library/blbioarchimedes.htm

www.technologystudent.com/joints/bolt1.htm

www.edheads.org/activities/simple-machines/

Printed in the U.S.A. — CG